BRAIN
STORMING

THE BOOK OF TOPICS

MART

Creative Learning Press, Inc.
P.O. Box 320, Mansfield Center, Connecticut 06250

ISBN: 0-936386-52-5

CONTENTS

INTRODUCTION

What a great joy it is to expand the mind so that it has a greater potential for processing information! Brainstorming is a unique procedure that stimulates the intellect. It is a learned skill—a cumulative process developed by practice over a period of time. Brainstorming involves the simultaneous processes of thinking, listening and responding.

Brainstorming teaches individuals to think comparatively, divergently and creatively. It is a technique to stretch the imagination and energize the mind. It becomes a challenging activity and a method for problem solving.

Actual measurement of mental growth is difficult; progress in brainstorming, however, can be observed over periods of time by working with the same group of individuals and video-taping or tape-recording sessions. These before-and-after recordings can be scrutinized for 1) variety of responses, 2) rapidity of responses, 3) uniqueness of ideas and 4) an increased complexity of ideas.

Who Should Brainstorm?

Brainstorming may be introduced to children as young as five. Brainstorming is also an appropriate activity for adults, and topics in this manual may be used for all ages. Even the easier Level I topics may generate innovative responses from adults, so these subjects should not be excluded as topics for mature brainstormers.

Level II topics are generally more difficult and are therefore suggested for older students. Keep in mind, however, that all topics in this book should be selected with knowledge of individual students and their abilities and interests. For example, you may find that some Level II topics are appropriate for elementary age students, and that some Level I topics can be used successfully with older students.

"I like brainstorming because I can share my imagination."

Student
Age 8

Getting Started

Instructions for the Leader

Brainstorming may be a planned or spontaneous activity. Any group of three or more individuals may participate; an ideal group size is five to seven. If more wish to brainstorm, teams may be formed. (Read further for team guidelines.)

The leader should select a quiet place since music, passing people, traffic noise and conversations are distractors. A carpeted area is ideal to muffle chair and foot noises. Have participants sit in a circle to ensure equality and to enable individuals to see and hear each other.

Select the topic and announce it to the group. Repeat it—with clarification, if necessary. Allow a one minute thinking time of silence during which those participating stockpile ideas. Suggest that this thinking time be used to list mentally five or six ideas so unique that no one else will think of them.

For example, if the brainstorming topic presented is to "name all the things you can think of that are green," an individual should skip the obvious ideas that would come to him readily, such as "trees," "grass" and a "magic marker." He would be better prepared by focusing on responses such as "greenback," "gangrene," "green with envy" and the song title "Greensleeves."

Ask participants to respond with one appropriate idea each time they have a turn. Participants are not to repeat what others have said or skip a turn. Once brainstorming has begun, all are quiet except for the one whose turn it is to speak. Each individual is to respond quickly and very briefly. Participants may not prompt one another. Each response should be only explicit enough to convey the general idea. Providing detail takes precious time from the timed activity.

If a participant repeats an idea previously mentioned, merely say, "Repeat," indicating to the speaker that the idea has already been expressed. The participant then responds with another idea.

The leader does not respond to ideas generated by the participants with enthusiasm or disapproval. As long as an idea is even loosely associated with the topic, it should be accepted. Such freedom of acceptance encourages off-the-wall, extremely original, weird and off-beat ideas. These are often the truly creative responses.

Turns progress clockwise around the circle. A three minute period is an ideal length of time for one topic. Have an egg timer or stop watch handy, and start it immediately after the one minute thinking time is over.

Watch the time-keeping device closely, but keep it out of the visual range of the brainstormers, as they tend to be distracted by watching the time pass, and during this distraction no ideas are generated.

Keeping score is one method of recording growth over a period of time. Scores may be kept for individuals, groups or teams. The simplest way of keeping score for an individual is to make a mark on a paper each time the person responds. However, for a group or team, with the participants seated in a circle, it is simpler to tally one mark for every round of responses. At the end of the three minute period, merely multiply the number of tallies by the number of individuals brainstorming and add in the number of responses given in the round before the time ran out.

A typical brainstorming session follows a systematic procedure. After the leader announces the topic and actual response time begins, an avalanche of ideas will come forth. This is the clearing stage, a time of getting the obvious ideas out of the mind. A plateau stage will likely follow, with few ideas generated or absolute quiet while additional thinking takes place. After this plateau stage, the truly creative, innovative period begins. An abundance of outstanding ideas will come forth. This is the most fascinating and exciting time for both the leader and participants.

A Practice Session

To familiarize participants with the brainstorming procedure, the leader can try some practice sessions using the following format. A subject is introduced and the leader makes certain that everyone fully understands the topic. Allow a one minute thinking time and then have participants raise their hands when they have an idea. Merely nod toward the individual wishing to respond. The procedure encourages rapid, brief, specific responses, provides a relatively relaxed atmosphere, and builds both confidence and enthusiasm.

The following tape-recorded session demonstrates a typical presentation of directions by the leader and actual student responses for a class of third graders. Eight children participated.

Leader: Class, after I give you your subject, you will have one minute to think, and then you will have three minutes in which to share your ideas. Whenever you have an idea to share, raise your hand. Your subject today is to complete this sentence, "I promise I'll...". What do you sometimes use as promises? These can be promises you make at school, at home, to your parents, to your friends, and so on. Again, the subject is to complete this sentence, "I promise I'll...". Are there any questions about the topic? *(Pause for student response.)* You now have one minute for thinking time.

Mandy: Do we have to repeat the first words each time?

Leader: No, do not repeat the first words. That would take too much of your time.

> *Begin one minute quiet thinking time.*
> *Participants may not help or coach one another.*

Leader: Your thinking time is over. We are ready to begin.

> *The Leader sets the timer.*

Tyler: Take out the trash.

Mandy: Set the table.

Molly: Clean my room.

Jamie: Play with my sister.

Bill: Feed the dog.

Heather: Be nice.

John: Weed the garden.

Jessica: I'll call you.

Jamie: Wash my hair.

Mandy: Will keep my promises.

Tyler: Go to the store for you.

Heather: Play quietly.

Molly: Help with supper.

Bill: Eat my bologna sandwich.

Jessica: Sweep the floor.

Tyler: Write my name on all my papers.

Bill: Flush the john.

Molly: Be good.

Mandy: Take a bath.

John: Play a game with you.

Jamie: Wash the dishes.

Mandy:	Clean my room.
	Pause
Jamie:	Return your pencil.
Jessica:	Turn out the lights.
Molly:	Make my bed every day.
Tyler:	Eat my dinner.
John:	Shut the door.
Bill:	Write to you every day.
Heather:	Put my bike away.

At this point there is a pause. The obvious responses have been cleared from the students' minds. This is the plateau stage. The ideas that follow the plateau stage are usually more divergent and creative.

Bill:	Won't forget my library books.
John:	Clean the mud from my shoes.
Mandy:	Whisper.
Molly:	Pay you back tomorrow.
Jamie:	Get up the first time you wake me.
Heather:	Take a real quick shower.
John:	Do all of my homework before supper.
Tyler:	Smile when you take my picture.
Molly:	Be home on time.
Bill:	Wear my glasses every day.

Mandy: Listen to directions.

Bill: Tell you a really funny joke.

Molly: Won't ever tell your secret.

John: Save all of my allowance.

Mandy: Never do it again.

Tyler: Give your diary back to you and never read it again.

Heather: Keep my eyes closed until you tell me to open them.

John: Never fight again.

Jessica: Go right to sleep.

Leader: The time is up. You have done an excellent job. Let's hear from those of you who had your hand up when the time ran out. *(By including these last ideas, the leader permits these individuals to share their last thoughts rather than squelch or disregard them, and this assures the students that all of their ideas will be accepted. Therefore, in future brainstorming sessions, they will continue to think of ideas until the very last instant.)*

Molly: Take care of a pet all by myself.

Tyler: Keep the stereo turned down really low.

Mandy: Get some sleep at my slumber party.

Bill: Clean up my own mess.

Leader: Those were some good additions. I want to compliment all of you for doing a fine job on this topic.

Skill Development

The leader may do a number of things to improve the skill and stimulate creativity within a regular group. Individuals should participate at least twice a week. Schedule the brainstorming sessions at various times of the day to determine peak levels of accelerated thought process for the group.

Use different types of topics. For example, if brainstorming takes place twice a week, select a topic from "Level I" for the first session and a "Sentence Completion" type the next time. Then choose a "Comparison" topic and after that have "One Minute" competitions. This variety maintains interest and develops a range of skills.

Becoming more creative in responding requires participants to utilize several techniques. If the topic presented is an object, consider what can be done with it if it is enlarged or made smaller. For example, a toothpick may become a needle or a minute hand on a watch when made smaller and a chop stick or telephone pole when made larger!

Another technique is to break an object into small pieces or rearrange the parts of it. For example, the lead in a pencil may be taken out and the wooden part used as a straw, or the wooden part may be chopped into small pieces, those pieces enlarged and then used as tunnels for children to play in!

Often one response will trigger an idea for another person. This is called *hitching* or *piggy-backing*. In this process, one person's idea stimulates the thought processes of another. Returning to the example of the lead pencil, after one person suggests the tunnel idea for children, another might continue the development of this idea and respond by cutting the tunnel in half and using the parts as animal watering troughs.

Brainstorming provides an opportunity for individuals to share their thoughts, to be creative and to learn from each other. In every brainstorming session, groups generate a multitude of ideas—many more than one individual could possibly produce!

Variations of Brainstorming:
Competitive Sessions

Team Competition	Have one team leave the room while the other team brainstorms. Give both teams the same topic. Keep time and tally responses. The team with the most responses wins.
Team Competition with More than Two Teams	Have members gather in groups in various places in the room. Provide each team with paper and several pencils. Establish which team member will be the secretary. Announce the topic to the entire room of people so that all team members hear it at the same time. The one minute thinking time follows. When competition begins, the team members tell their secretary their ideas and these are written down on the paper. At the end of the time period, responses are counted. Watch for duplications, as in the haste of recording responses some ideas may be repeated. The time period for this activity may be extended by one or two minutes because writing down ideas slows the process.

This activity is really a challenge! Have one member of a team leave the room. Give the topic to those team members remaining and give them one minute to think. The team member then returns, listens to the responses and tries to guess the topic, breaking in at any time he feels he knows the subject. The three minute time period is not used here, but participants may agree on calling it a forfeit after a certain amount of time or a certain number of responses have been given. The winning team is the one that guesses the topic in the least number of responses.

Double Brain-storming

This game involves two or more teachers exchanging students. Teams are formed with students from each class. Each student brainstorms twice, once with each teacher. This is an ideal opportunity for students to socialize with those from other classes and to get acquainted with other teachers. It is also an opportunity for students to hear the types of responses given by those older and younger than themselves.

Class Exchange

The Buddy Approach

This is good for developing speed and skill. In groups of two, each member writes down one brainstorming topic. Both topics are placed face down and exchanged. One team member picks up the topic, reads it and has one minute in which to think. The three minute time period begins and the buddy keeps score. The roles are then reversed, and a winner is declared. A third person may write down the topics, keep score, and be the time keeper.

Beat Yourself

Teams begin with a topic and brainstorm for three minutes in the usual manner. The leader keeps score and then introduces a second topic, preferably one related to the first. Compare the score from the first and second topics. The goal is to surpass the number of responses given for the first topic. Here are some related topics:

Junk foods
Foods that are good for you

Things that are hot
Things that are cold

An excuse
A law or rule

Where in the world would you find salt?
Where in the world would you find water?

Variations of Brainstorming: Other Types of Sessions

Place many different brainstorming topics in a jar or box. Have one participant reach in and select a topic, sight unseen. That individual then has one minute of thinking time before responding. A response time of two minutes is ideal for this activity. Score is kept. Then another participant selects a topic and the procedure is repeated until each has had a turn. The winner, of course, is the one with the highest number of responses.

Pick a Topic

Object Usage is another approach that lends itself to a multitude of creative responses. Pass an object around without supplying any identifiable information. Ask participants to tell what the object could be used for. Antique kitchen gadgets or parts of farm equipment are ideal for this.

Object Usage

In this game, any number of individuals may participate, and all are seated in a circle. The leader announces the subject, and the one-minute thinking time follows. Going around the circle, each participant responds with one idea. There is no time limit for this game; however, if an individual responds with an idea that has already been mentioned, the leader says, "Out," and that person is no longer in the game. Also, if a participant takes over ten seconds to respond, he is out. The last person remaining becomes the winner!

Last Man Wins!

Alphabet Brainstorming

Alphabet Brainstorming is for the more advanced brainstormer. The leader begins with any word, and each participant must respond with a word that begins with either the first letter or the last letter of the word given by the leader. Thus the letter changes with each response. A participant cannot think ahead. This is a difficult technique but ideal for developing thinking and processing skills. For example, given the word "pen," the first person may respond with a word that begins with either the letter "p" or "n." If the response is "nail," the next person may give a word that begins with either the letter "n" or "l." As this process takes a little more thinking time, the three-minute period may be extended.

Word Building

Word Building is the building on either the first or second word of a compound word. For example, given the word "houseboat," the next participant may respond with a compound word built on either "house" or "boat" such as "playhouse" or "speedboat." In this game one may not stockpile ideas during a thinking period, so that step is omitted. Some good words to begin with for this are "garage door," "leapfrog," "baby-sitter," high chair," and "kingpin."

REMINDERS

- Never allow brainstorming to become routine

- Vary the types of topics

- Vary the response time

- Vary the time of day for brainstorming

- Rotate individuals from one team to another

- BE CREATIVE! HAVE FUN!

Samples of Responses

Where in the world would you find a leaf or leaves?

on a Canadian flag

Leif Erickson

on a postage stamp

as a cake decoration

in a museum

on a calendar

pressed in a book

on a rug

blown in the garage

in a bedroll

on a microscope slide

in a collection

in a trash bag

imprinted on a coin

in a movie

a table leaf

caught on a rake

used as a bookmark

a word in a book

stuck on a windshield wiper

in your imagination

in a compost pile

in an animal cage

turn over a new leaf

burning leaves

on the porch

Hawaiian skirt made of ti leaves

"Autumn Leaves" song title

Give as many uses as you can think of for a piece of construction paper.

make a mobile

confetti

fold it into a hat

book cover

make a fan

place mat

book mark

crumple it up for a ball

wallpaper

make a tube

envelope

fold like a box for jewelry

baby bib

wrapping paper

cut numbers or letters out of it

buy it

throw it away

burn it

sell it

make it into a page for an album

blow your nose in it

make a calendar page out of it

make a sign or poster

make an airplane

cut it in strips and make a chain

make a card

rip it

make a checker board

use it as the face of a clock

make a Christmas tree ornament

cut out paper doll clothes

make finger prints on it

make a mask

weave with it

laminate it

make a name tag

play tic-tac-toe on it

tear it to make mosaic designs

use it as a napkin

make it into a paper bag

make play glasses to wear

step on it

make an apron

make spit balls

cut it to make a jigsaw puzzle

shred it

put sticky stuff on it to make fly paper

use it for paper-mache

stuff it into a shoe that is too big

make an eye patch

make it into streamers

make Indian feathers

use it for origami

line a mouse nest with pieces

cut out the center and use as a picture frame

make a teepee

carpet a doll house

make paper money

enlarge it and use it as a table cloth

roll it and use it as a telescope

design it and use it as a postage stamp

cut out a snowflake

make a doll diaper

use it for a menu cover

cut for a file card

make a sun visor

use it as a page of a book

line an animal's cage with it

make a deck of cards

use it as a roof over a log cabin house

use it as a chalkboard

use it as a coaster

LISTS OF TOPICS

General Topics—Level I

Name things that have holes in them _____

Give uses for a balloon _____

Give uses for a baby's bib _____

Name things that will roll _____

Give uses for a rubber band _____

Name things that have seeds in them _____

Give uses for a piece of toast _____

Give uses for an empty snail shell _____

Give uses for a typewriter key _____

Give uses for a postage stamp _____

Give uses for a raisin _____

Give uses for an ice cube _____

Name things you might find in a pond _____

Give uses for a trash can lid _____

Give uses for snow _____

Name an occupation _____

Name an animal that lives on a farm _____

Give uses for a cowboy's pistol _____

Give uses for an M & M _____

General Topics—Level I

Date Used

_____ Give uses for an empty aspirin bottle

_____ Name a kind of sandwich

_____ Give uses for a staple

_____ Name a tool used for work

_____ Name things made of cloth

_____ Name things you can wear on your head

_____ Name a kind of soup

_____ Name an animal that lives in a pond, river or lake

_____ Name anything that fastens things together

_____ Name things in a house that hold other things *(examples: a candlestick holds a candle, a drawer holds silverware)*

_____ Give uses for a grain of sand

_____ Name things that you can open

_____ Name things that live in a jungle

_____ Name a part of a car

_____ Name a breakfast cereal

_____ Name an animal you might find in your house

_____ Name things you might find in a treasure chest

General Topics—Level I

Date Used

Name ways to have fun _____

Give uses for a cup _____

Give uses for a hair ribbon _____

Give uses for a car hood ornament _____

Give uses for a seed _____

Give uses for ashes from a fireplace _____

Give uses for an empty egg shell _____

Name things you might do with a glove _____

Give uses for a windshield wiper _____

Name things you might do on a day that _____
school is cancelled

Give uses for a recipe file box _____

Name things you consider beautiful _____

Name a wild animal _____

Name things you might hang from _____
a necklace

Name things you use in school _____

Name a machine in your house _____

Name things that are square _____

Name things you can wash _____

General Topics—Level I

_____ Name things you can juggle

_____ Give uses for a paper clip

_____ Name things that grow

_____ Name things that are white

_____ Name things you can throw

_____ Name things that hold food

_____ Give a word with a double letter *(examples: apple, little)*

_____ Name things you can do with your feet

_____ Name words that begin with the letter *s*

_____ Name something you can hold in your hand

_____ Name things you can knock over

_____ Name things you can step on

_____ Give uses for a pencil

_____ Name things that go bump in the night

_____ Give uses for a toothpick

_____ Name things that are round

_____ Name things that break

_____ Name things you might find in a bathroom medicine cabinet

General Topics—Level I

Name things you might find in a lunch box _____

Name things that make a sound when they _____
are dropped

Name things that stretch _____

Name things you can turn _____

Name things you can wear _____

Name things that are considered fragile _____
(examples: feelings, a butterfly wing)

Name things you can pick up with _____
a crochet hook

Name anything you can shake _____

Name things you might find in _____
a picnic basket

Give uses for the cardboard under pizza _____

Name things you find in the ground _____

Name anything you might see in a parade _____

Give uses for a pie pan _____

Give uses for a shingle from a roof _____

Name things you might find in a basement _____

Name anything you can poke holes into _____

Name things that have wings _____

27

General Topics—Level I

_____ Name things that can be thrown away

_____ Name things the wind can blow

_____ Give uses for a beanbag

_____ Name things that bounce

_____ Give uses for a candy Life-Saver

_____ Give uses for a screwdriver

_____ Give uses for a Q-tip

_____ Give uses for a wooden clothes pin

_____ Give uses for a pipe cleaner

_____ Give uses for a paper towel tube

_____ Name things you might do with
a Hershey's Kiss

_____ Give uses for a string of pearls

_____ Give uses for a funnel

_____ Give uses for an old map

_____ Give uses for a jigsaw puzzle piece

_____ Name anything related to a boat

_____ Name anything a gardener might use

_____ Name things found in the kitchen

General Topics—Level I

General Topics—Level I

_____ Give uses for a fork

_____ Give uses for charcoal

_____ Give uses for a spool from thread

_____ Give uses for the top of a turtle shell

_____ Give uses for a drinking straw

_____ Give uses for a nail

_____ Give uses for a phonograph record

_____ Give uses for pencil lead

_____ Give uses for a marble

_____ Give uses for a blank piece of paper

_____ Give uses for a button

_____ Give uses for a light bulb

_____ Name a sound you hear every day

_____ Give uses for a cup of water

_____ Name a food eaten at breakfast

_____ Name something to drink

_____ Name things that have water in them

_____ Give uses for a ten-inch piece of rope

_____ Give uses for a belt

General Topics—Level I

Name things made of leather _____

Name things made of wood _____

Name a word with an *s* in it that is not the _____
first or last letter of the word

Name things that have wheels _____

Name things that make you feel good _____

Give uses for a book _____

Name a kind of snack _____

Name things you might bring to school _____
(example: measles)

Name things that have spots _____

Name things you can write with _____

Name things you can rip or tear _____

Name things that are slippery _____

Name things that are shiny _____

Name things that are sweet _____

Name things that are salty _____

Name things that are sour _____

Give uses for a playing card _____

Give uses for one die _____

General Topics—Level I

_____ Name things you can give away

_____ Name things that fly

_____ Name things that crawl

_____ Give uses for a penny

_____ Give uses for a chalkboard eraser

_____ Give uses for a soup can

_____ Give uses for half of a tennis ball

_____ Give uses for a key

_____ Give uses for a comb

_____ Give uses for a milk carton

_____ Name things you can catch

_____ Name things that leave a mark

_____ Name things that are white

_____ Name a TV star

_____ Name an object operated by a battery

_____ Name things that are warm to the touch

_____ Name things you can walk on

_____ Give uses for an old sheet or blanket

_____ Name things that float

General Topics—Level I

Date Used

Name things that are cold _____

Name things that have a flat surface _____

Give uses for a dollar bill _____

Name an animal that has a tail _____

Name things you might plant in a garden _____

Name a song _____

Give the name of a kind of tree _____

Name a kind of flower _____

Name things that are out of place _____
in your bedroom

Name things you can make music with _____

Give uses for a cake of soap _____

Name things that need to be trimmed _____

Give uses for sandpaper _____

Give uses for an old picture frame _____

Give uses for a match _____

Give uses for an umbrella _____

Give uses for sawdust _____

Name anything that might fit _____
in a ring box

General Topics—Level I

_____ Name things you might take in your knapsack on a ten-mile hike (Remember, you have to carry it!)

_____ Name things for which you might use a pair of scissors

_____ Name things made of styrofoam

_____ Give uses for a pillow

_____ Give uses for a paint chip like those found in paint stores

_____ Give uses for a paint brush

_____ Give uses for a pop can

_____ Give uses for a cotton ball

_____ Give uses for a china dinner plate

_____ Give uses for wrapping paper

_____ Give uses for a snap

_____ Name things made of gold

_____ Give uses for a book bag

_____ Give uses for a tennis racket

_____ Name things you might cut with a knife

_____ Give uses for a sponge

_____ Give uses for a golf ball

General Topics—Level I

Date Used

Give uses for an eraser _____

Give uses for an old calendar _____

Give uses for a domino _____

Give uses for a sock _____

Give uses for a wig _____

Give uses for a bottle cap _____

Give uses for a hubcap _____

Give uses for a candle stick _____

Give uses for a paper doily _____

Give uses for a fly swatter _____

Name things you might trace around _____

Give uses for a cookie cutter _____

Give uses for knee pads _____

Give uses for a hat _____

Give uses for earmuffs _____

Name things you might use as a hopscotch _____
marker (or a game piece)

Give uses for a pan lid _____

Name things out of which you could make _____
confetti

General Topics—Level I

_____ Name things with which you can dig

_____ Name objects you might use as a flour scoop

_____ Name something with which you could hit someone on the head

_____ Give uses for an old shoe (example: plant flowers in it)

_____ Give uses for an old bathtub or sink plug

_____ Give uses for a paddle

_____ Give uses for a strainer

_____ Name things you might use for a base in a game of baseball

_____ Name things you might pass in a relay race

_____ Name things you might fill with candy *(yes, an amphitheater!)*

_____ Give uses for a yo-yo

_____ Name things that are red

_____ Give uses for a twelve-inch ruler

_____ Give uses for a shoestring

_____ Give uses for a stone

_____ Name things that are blue

_____ Give uses for a nutcracker

General Topics—Level I

Date Used

Give uses for an old license plate _____

Give uses for hands on a clock _____

Give uses for a paper towel _____

Give uses for a coffee can lid _____

Give uses for a comb _____

Give uses for a plastic garbage bag _____

Give uses for pliers for _____

Give uses for an envelope _____

Give uses for a doorknob _____

Give uses for window screening _____

Give uses for a baseball cap _____

Name things you might use as _____
a book mark

Give uses for a bead _____

Give uses for ten inches of wire _____

Give uses for a crutch _____

Give uses for a camera case _____

Give uses for a dandelion _____

Name things you might do with _____
soggy cereal

General Topics—Level I

_____ Give uses for a flower pot

_____ Name things that you might put in a salad

_____ Give uses for a Ping-Pong ball

_____ Give uses for a piece of hose

_____ Name things you might carry
a grasshopper in

_____ Name a cookie ingredient

_____ Give a girl's name

_____ Give a boy's name

_____ Name a kind of dog (examples: hot dog,
watch dog, hound dog, dog face)

_____ Name a piece of camping equipment

_____ Give the exact title of a book

_____ Name a word that begins with the letter r

_____ Name an outdoor game

_____ Name a part of the body

_____ Give uses for a feather

_____ Name things you could find in a bakery

_____ Give uses for a long piece of spaghetti

_____ Give uses for a pillow case

General Topics—Level I

Date Used

Name things you can squeeze _____

Give uses for a carpet square _____

Give uses for a front door _____

Name utensils or objects which you might use to eat ice cream _____

Give uses for a sheet of paper _____

Give uses for a Band-Aid _____

Name a fairy tale character _____

Name things that crunch when you eat them _____

Name an insect _____

Give uses for a golf tee _____

Name a part of an airplane _____

Name things that fly _____

Name a musical instrument _____

Name things you might see in an airport _____

Give uses for a twist from a bread wrapper _____

Name a kind of candy _____

Name things you can kick _____

Give uses for a marshmallow _____

General Topics—Level I

_____ Give uses for a fingernail file

_____ Name a kind of license

_____ Name things that have knobs

_____ Give uses for a man's necktie

_____ Give uses for a towel

_____ Name things you can do with a golf club

_____ Give uses for a bedroll

_____ Name things you might wrap yourself in
to keep warm

_____ Give uses for an old sweat shirt

_____ Name things that are sticky

_____ Name a food that comes in a can

_____ Give uses for grass clippings

_____ Name things people collect

_____ Give uses for a carpet square

_____ Give any word or thing related
to the theater

_____ Give uses for a Frisbee

_____ Name things held together with nails

_____ Name ways to cut down a tree

General Topics—Level I

Date Used

Name things that are hard to give away ⎯⎯⎯⎯

Give uses for a shoe box ⎯⎯⎯⎯

Name things you can balance on ⎯⎯⎯⎯
your finger

Name things you can cut with scissors ⎯⎯⎯⎯

Name things you can read ⎯⎯⎯⎯

Name things that will fit in a walnut shell ⎯⎯⎯⎯

Name a place to visit ⎯⎯⎯⎯

Name things on which you can sit ⎯⎯⎯⎯

Name things you can tie in a knot ⎯⎯⎯⎯

Name places to read a magazine ⎯⎯⎯⎯

Give a reason for not keeping a dental ⎯⎯⎯⎯
appointment

Name something that gives you ⎯⎯⎯⎯
a headache

Give uses for gravel from a fish tank ⎯⎯⎯⎯

Name ways to spend one dollar ⎯⎯⎯⎯

Name things you might find in a kitchen ⎯⎯⎯⎯
cupboard

Name a dessert ⎯⎯⎯⎯

Name a place to walk ⎯⎯⎯⎯

General Topics—Level I

Date Used

_____ Name things you could drill a hole into

_____ Name things you might find in a bathroom medicine cabinet

_____ Name places where might you find a clock

_____ Give uses for an eye patch

_____ Give uses for a cork

_____ Name things you might put in an envelope

_____ Give uses for a telephone book

_____ Name things you might put in a styrofoam cup

_____ Give some wishes people make

_____ Name a kind of sports equipment

_____ Name things that have sugar in them

_____ Name ways to blaze a trail

_____ Name things you might put in a picture frame

_____ Name foods you eat with your fingers

_____ Name reasons moms get mad at kids

_____ Name a place to hide

_____ Name a dessert

_____ Name a characteristic of a friend

General Topics—Level I

Name an item in a salad bar   _____

Name things a vacuum cleaner might pick up   _____

Name something you would see in a museum   _____

Name things that are painted   _____

Name things that spill   _____

Name ways to get down a hill   _____

Name things to do with a potato   _____

Name things people watch   _____

Name ways to pass time while waiting in a doctor's office   _____

General Topics—Level II

Name ways to get to sleep _____

Give a word (make one up) that nobody has _____
ever heard of

Give a word that describes sadness _____

Name a kind of ring _____

Name a place to visit *(examples: park,* _____
resort, camp)

Name a word that ends in *-ly* _____

Dolls, long ago, were made of sticks. _____
Name other things out of which
dolls could be made

Name things that come in pairs _____

Name things that tell you to stop _____

Name things that soak up other things _____

Name things that stretch across something _____
(examples: a bridge, a rubber band,
a clothes line)

Give a verb _____

Give a slang word _____

Give a foreign language phrase _____
(examples: etc., RSVP)

Make up a word and give it a meaning _____

General Topics—Level II

_____ Name a freedom

_____ Name states in alphabetical order *(once a state has been named, a participant may not name a state that comes earlier in the alphabet.)*

_____ Name things on which you can carve

_____ Name things you can do to another person

_____ Name a famous person

_____ Name things you can see through

_____ Name a brand and a product (example: Hoover—vacuum cleaner; Kodak—film)

_____ Name things that absorb sound

_____ Give uses for a mirror

_____ Name things that have a handle

_____ Name a kind of travel

_____ Tell a superstition

_____ Give an adjective

_____ Name a law

_____ Give uses for a shield

_____ Name a kind of measurement

_____ Name a famous author

General Topics—Level II

Give uses for Velcro _____

Name a city _____

Name things that have stripes _____

Name a word that describes a sound _____
(examples: clunk, sizzle)

Name a feeling _____

Give ways to put out a dragon's fire _____

Name things that make you angry _____

Name things that need each other _____

Give uses for an apple corer _____

Name a game people play _____

Give an excuse *(Examples: I didn't think you* _____
meant me! I'm too tired.
He hit me first.)

Name things that drop _____

Name something you would pack in a _____
suitcase for a trip

Give uses for tough beef jerky _____

Give uses for a microscope slide _____

Name things you could do with lint from a _____
clothes dryer

47

General Topics—Level II

_____ Name a body of water

_____ Give uses for a credit card

_____ Name an inventor or explorer

_____ Give uses for dental floss

_____ Name things that make you sad

_____ Give an emergency sound or word

_____ Name a country

_____ Name a river

_____ Name a high school course of study

_____ Name a kind of rock *(example: Rock of Gibraltar, Rock Hudson, don't rock the boat)*

_____ Name a disease

_____ Name a word that ends with *-ology (example: mythology, psychology, biology)*

_____ Name an occupation

_____ Give uses for a thimble

_____ Give uses for wet coffee grounds

_____ Give uses for a computer floppy disk

_____ Give a cliché *(examples: strong as an ox, sky-high)*

General Topics—Level II

Give uses for a piece of cheese cloth   _____

Give uses for a melon baller   _____

Name things that are soft to the touch   _____

Name a nocturnal animal   _____

Name a kind of doctor   _____

Give a four syllable word   _____

Name something you can ride   _____

Name a place where an animal lives   _____

Name things that absorb sound   _____

Give two rhyming words   _____

Name things you can drive over (in a car)   _____
and not really hurt

Name things that bounce   _____

Give uses for a shoehorn   _____

Name a college or university   _____

Name things you can catch   _____

Name a Greek or Roman god or goddess   _____

Give an advertising slogan *(examples:*   _____
*Things go better with Coke. You'll be
happier with a Hoover.)*

General Topics—Level II

_____ Name a place to sleep *(Note that this is not limited to humans, but let participants discover this.)*

_____ Things you might buy at a flea market.

_____ Give uses for a crochet hook.

_____ Name something you plug into an electrical outlet

_____ Name things you can peel

_____ Name a sign you might see on the side of the road

_____ Tell of a way to lose weight

_____ Name an important historical event

_____ Sing the first line of a song

_____ Give a five letter word

_____ Name a magazine

_____ Name things you might time with a stopwatch

_____ Name things you could program your own robot to do

_____ Name things that bend

_____ Name things you can look through

_____ Name kinds of money used anywhere in the world

General Topics—Level II

Name things you can cut _____

Name a kind of communication _____

Name a cartoon character _____

Give uses for an elephant tusk _____

Give uses for a tea bag _____

Name things you can eat with a spoon _____

Name a college or university _____

What do the letters "C.B." stand for? _____
(Examples: Charlie Brown,
cute baby, cruel brother)

Name a five letter word with a consonant in _____
the middle

Give an adjective and noun that alliterate _____
(Exampes: better butter, perfect party,
dumb dress)

Sentence Completion

You might flip a coin to determine... _____

Love is like... _____

As quick as... _____

In January it was so cold that... _____

I grew up in a town so small that... _____

My little black book contains... _____

You could catch a falling star by... _____

I'm absolutely sincere when I say... _____

Seeing you makes me feel... _____

I promise I'll... _____

I spent a great weekend... _____

I answered the telephone and my _____
mother said...

I really get nervous when... _____

I get butterflies in my stomach when... _____

On the kitchen table is... _____

The light was out and I tripped over... _____

I didn't get milk at the store because... _____

When the film was developed, I had a _____
picture of...

53

Sentence Completion

_____ I could become famous by…

_____ In the mail yesterday I received…

_____ Reflected in the mirror I saw…

_____ It is really easy because…

_____ A letter was mailed, but never received because…

_____ A bottle washed up on the shore with a note inside that said…

_____ I don't have my homework today because…

_____ Opening the picnic basket, I saw…

_____ There is a scratch on your face that got there by…

_____ Here is check for $10.00 for…

_____ I found a spider web…

_____ On my submarine sandwich I put…

_____ Today my pet dog…

_____ The radio announcer said…

_____ Since I can't find the rolling pin, I will flatten the dough by…

_____ It won't be long now until…

Sentence Completion

I found a note on my desk that said... _____

Instead of money, the tooth fairy left... _____

In the soup I found... _____

Something I don't know how to cook is... _____

The suitcase absolutely would not close, so I... _____

On the file card I wrote... _____

A letter was mailed, but never received because... _____

A bottle washed up on the shore with a note inside that said... _____

I don't have my homework done today because... _____

For a trip to Florida I would pack... _____

My hair is straight today because... _____

I'm wearing two different socks today because... _____

I broke my arm... _____

The principal at our school has not shown up at a meeting. She was detained because... _____

Sentence Completion

What Would Happen If...?

_____ If there were no animals...

_____ If there were no cars...

_____ If there were no telephones...

_____ If there were no such things as maps...

_____ If there were no names...

_____ If we couldn't talk...

_____ If there were no sickness...

_____ If everybody was bald (consider professions involved,... adornments for the hair, etc.)

_____ If there were no pencils, pens, chalk, crayons, etc.

_____ If there were no noise...

_____ If there were no commercials...

_____ If there were no nighttime...

_____ If we didn't have a president...

_____ If we had three arms...

_____ If there were no alphabet...

_____ If all cars were the same color...

Sentence Completion

If there were no rules... _____

If man ate no meat... _____

If a family could have only one child... _____

If the sun never shined on Sundays... _____

If it didn't cost anything to mail a letter... _____

If there were a pill you could take to _____
make you live 500 years... *(Consider;
would it be available to everyone or only
you? Could you take half a pill? etc.)*

If there were no such thing as odor... _____

If everyone moved every year... _____

If you were born grown up... _____

If there were no such thing as glass... _____

If people were not allowed to move... _____

If nobody slept... _____

If we had no clocks... _____

If cars were made of brick... _____

If my parents had to spend a week in _____
school with me every year...

If I had no thumb... _____

Sentence Completion

_____ If we had no teeth...

_____ If there were no junk food...

_____ If lands were not separated by water...

One Minute Topics

Name things you can pick up with a pair of tweezers　_____

Name something to put on a hat to decorate it　_____

Name things that you might find in your freezer　_____

Name things you can boil　_____

Name ways to cool off　_____

Name things that might give you a headache　_____

Give a title of an office or rank　_____

Name reasons to oversleep　_____

Name things you can tie to make a bow or knot　_____

Name a game that uses dice　_____

Name a way to lose weight　_____

Name a way to keep score　_____

Name a good name for a dog　_____

Name a way to get rich　_____

Name things that feel rough　_____

Name things that are left in pockets and go through the washer　_____

One Minute Topics

_____ Name objects that could be used as a paperweight

_____ Name things to drink on a hot day

_____ Name cookie ingredients

_____ Name advertisements found in home beautification magazines

_____ Give names of states

_____ Name a bird *(example: an early bird!)*

_____ Name childrens' outdoor games

_____ Name snack foods

_____ Give words that begin with the letter *x*

_____ Name a book title

_____ Name kinds of cereals

_____ Name countries

_____ Name things to make with ground beef

_____ Name things to use as Christmas ornaments

_____ Give brand names

_____ Name an article of clothing

_____ Give a two-syllable word

_____ Name kinds of measurement

One Minute Topics

Name things inside the body _____

Name things you can hit to make _____
a drum-like noise

Name places you want to visit _____

Name things you might do in a gymn _____

Name things you might put in a sandwich _____

Name things you might send _____
in an envelope

Name good places to put a light bulb _____

Name things you might put in your _____
washing machine

Name things that burn _____

Name things you can put in your mouth _____

Name ways to shade yourself from _____
the sun

Name an island _____

Give the name of a war or battle _____

Name a color _____

Name a cooking style *(example:* _____
Mexican, Basque, French)

Give a last name _____

One Minute Topics

_____ Name a bad habit

_____ Give a word ending in -meter *(examples: pentameter, odometer, pedometer)*

_____ Name things found in a can

_____ Name things you might find on the bottom of your shoe

_____ Name kinds of cats

_____ Name things that run on or have wheels

_____ Name a four-legged animal

_____ Name things that produce heat

_____ Name a body process *(examples: breathing, digestion, sleeping, dreaming)*

_____ Name things you can tie in a knot or bow

_____ Name things you can read *(examples: menu, an instrument, insurance policy)*

_____ Name things you might celebrate

_____ Name a sport

_____ Name things you might use as an anchor

_____ Name things that snap when they break

_____ Name a kind of medicine

_____ Name things you can squeeze

One Minute Topics

Name things that wear out _____

Name things with moveable parts _____

Name things that are free _____

Name things that go up and down _____

Name sounds you hear in the kitchen *(ex-* _____
amples: food frying, ice maker)

Use the following word in as many ways as you can:

egg _____
(examples: fried, coddled, egg on your face, exaggerate, excuse, scrambled, benedict, dumplings, noodles, rolls, sandwich, salad, plant, not, deviled, foo-young, hard-boiled, omelet, shirred, souffle.)

high _____

water _____

spring _____

city _____

ring _____

roll _____

apple _____

light _____

One Minute Topics

_____ Name a method of waking someone

_____ Name things you can use to make a book cover

_____ Give uses for a three-minute egg timer

_____ Name things that have knobs you can turn

_____ Name things you can hang on a wall

_____ Give uses for nail polish

_____ Name a game you play with dice

_____ Give a kind of measurement

_____ Name a kind of sign

_____ Name things you can mash

_____ Name things you might wrap around a spool

_____ Name a place to run

_____ Name places grass will grow

_____ Name things you might use to fan yourself on a hot day

_____ Name reasons to have a party

_____ Name places you might find a toothbrush

_____ Name a musical term

_____ Name things you might hang from a mobile

One MinuteTopics

Name things that are bright _____

Name things that smell bad _____

Name an adjective that describes Grandpa _____

Name things kept in a safe deposit box _____

Give uses for aluminum foil _____

Name things that make you sad _____

Name a kind of exercise _____

Name a bad habit _____

Name jobs for which people have to wear _____
uniforms

Name things you might want to shred _____

Name things you can drink through a straw _____

Name ways to scratch your back _____

Name ways to make people laugh _____

Holiday & Seasonal Topics

Valentine's Day

Date Used

_____ Words on a candy heart might say...

_____ Besides a card, another way to send a valentine is...

_____ Name things you could do with an old valentine

Easter

_____ Give as many uses as you can think of for a jelly bean

_____ Give uses for artificial grass

_____ Give uses for Easter egg shells

Halloween

_____ You could make a mask out of...

_____ Give uses for a pumpkin seed

_____ Feeling the inside of a pumpkin reminds me of...

_____ For Halloween, I'd like to be...

Thanksgiving

_____ On Thanksgiving Day I will...

_____ Between now and Christmas, I will be...

_____ With a turkey bone I could...

Holiday & Seasonal Topics

Date Used

I am thankful for... _____

Name things you could make from a corn husk _____

Name things you could make or do with a _____
turkey feather

Christmas

Right now Santa is busy... _____

On Christmas morning, I wish... _____

In my stocking I would like to find... _____

Name things that are red _____

Something I am glad did not happen on _____
Christmas Day is...

A gift I would really like to give _____
someone is...

Give uses for an old Christmas tree _____

Give uses for a Christmas tree _____
ornament hook

Give uses for leftover wrapping paper _____

Winter

A snowy day is a good time to... _____

Sitting in front of a fire, I think of... _____

Snow is good for... _____

Holiday & Seasonal Topics

Spring

_____ Name things that are green

_____ Name things that make you happy

_____ Name things the sun shines on

_____ Spring makes me think of...

Fall

_____ Fall leaves can be used to...

_____ Name an animal that is preparing for the winter

_____ Fall makes me think of...

Comparisons & Complexities

Name a manufactured item for each letter of
the alphabet *(example:* a—*abacus,* b—*block,*
c—*car, etc.)* _____

Your ship is sinking. What will you do? *(See if
students arrive at the implication they own
the ship and might not be on it.)* _____

The money you saved has disappeared.
What happened to it? _____

How many kinds of traps can you think of? _____

Name an object and then its motion *(examples:
car—skids; boat—rocks; radio—plays)* _____

Give a simile _____

Name pairs of words that sound the same but
are spelled differently *(example: rode, road;
buy by; two, to)* _____

Name things you can do that your
parents can't _____

Name things your parents can do that
you can't _____

There is a Mother's Day, Father's Day, etc.
What holiday would you create? _____

Name reasons why families move _____

Name things that cause a person to worry _____

Name a "white" lie _____

Comparisons & Complexities

Date Used

Compare

_____ a frog with a flower *(examples: both begin with f, both grow, both need water, both are relatively small, both have some green usually, etc.)*

_____ a pen with an owl

_____ a shoe with a fork

_____ an apple and a Coke bottle

_____ a camera and a book

_____ a jacket and a tree

_____ a telephone and a camera

_____ an electric cord and a coat hanger

_____ a marble and a piece of candy

_____ a chicken and a horse

Compare and Contrast

_____ a mask and a saddle

_____ a milkshake and a loaf of bread

_____ a violin and a stapler

Where Would You Find...?

	Date Used		Date Used
flowers	_____	stairs	_____
salt	_____	a suitcase	_____
water	_____	a stop watch	_____
palm trees	_____	a button	_____
a bit of oil	_____	a paperback book	_____
a piece of yarn	_____	a flashlight	_____
an aspirin	_____	a life jacket	_____
burning wood	_____	a photograph	_____
a cup of coffee	_____	an apple	_____
a knitting needle	_____	a leaf	_____
a match	_____	the President's name	_____
a marshmallow	_____	a dust rag	_____
a paper airplane	_____	a pencil	_____
a grandmother	_____	a spider	_____
a kitchen knife	_____	a love letter	_____
masking tape	_____	a teddy bear	_____
a ball	_____	carbon paper	_____
mustard	_____	a hair brush	_____
a newspaper	_____		

Where Would You Find...?

_____ a trumpet

_____ a quarter

_____ a tomato seed

_____ a roll of
Scotch Tape

_____ a pine cone

_____ a sponge

_____ a baseball

_____ a pair of
scissors

_____ a dictionary

_____ a fire ex-
tinguisher

_____ a magnifying glass

_____ an American flag

_____ a car key

_____ a shell

_____ a wallet

_____ a glove

_____ a rubber band

_____ popped corn

_____ a mask

_____ a photograph

_____ a dollar bill

Notes

Notes

Notes

Notes